02/
12

WILDFIRES

Paul Mason

A+

Smart Apple Media
P.O. Box 3263
Mankato, MN, 56002

First published in 2011 by
MACMILLAN EDUCATION AUSTRALIA PTY LTD
15–19 Claremont St, South Yarra, Australia 3141

Visit our web site at www.macmillan.com.au or go directly to www.macmillanlibrary.com.au

Associated companies and representatives throughout the world.

Library of Congress Cataloging-in-Publication Data has been applied for.

Publisher: Carmel Heron
Commissioning Editor: Niki Horin
Managing Editor: Vanessa Lanaway
Editors: Philip Bryan and Tim Clarke
Proofreader: Kylie Cockle
Designer: Cristina Neri, Canary Graphic Design
Page layout: Cristina Neri, Canary Graphic Design
Photo researcher: Jes Senbergs (management: Debbie Gallagher)
Illustrator: Peter Bull Art Studio
Production Controller: Vanessa Johnson

Manufactured in China by Macmillan Production (Asia) Ltd.
Kwun Tong, Kowloon, Hong Kong
Supplier Code: CP January 2011

Acknowledgments
The author and publisher are grateful to the following for permission to reproduce copyright material:

Front cover photograph: Residents run for their cars in a parking lot behind the Oakwood Apartments as
a wildfire burns in the Hollywood hills section of Los Angeles on Friday, March 30, 2007, courtesy of AAP
Image/AP/Mike Meadows.

Photographs courtesy of: CFA Strategic Communications. All rights reserved/Keith Packenham, **5**, /Keren
Freeman, **16**; Corbis/Nik Wheeler, **22**; Fema Photo/Andrea Booher, **28**, **29**, /Brian Dahlberg, **26**, /Bob
McMillan, **21**, /Michael Mancino, **14**; Getty Images/AFP, **23**; iStockPhoto/Simon Owler, **19**, /Wesley Tolhurst,
4, /Andreas Weber, **9**, /Michael Walker, **10**; Photolibrary, **18**, /David Inc, **11**, /NASA, **20**; Reuters/Mario
Anzugni, **12**, /Fred Greaves, **7**, /John Kolesidis, **27**, /Stringer Australia, **15**; Wikipedia, **13**.

While every care has been taken to trace and acknowledge copyright, the publisher tenders their apologies
for any accidental infringement where copyright has proved untraceable. They would be pleased to come to
a suitable arrangement with the rightful owner in each case.

CONTENTS

DISASTER WORDS

When a word is printed in **bold**, look for its meaning in the "Disaster Words" box.

DISASTER WATCH

Natural disasters can destroy whole areas and kill thousands of people. The only protection from them is to go on disaster watch. This means knowing the warning signs that a disaster might be about to happen, and having a plan for what to do if one strikes.

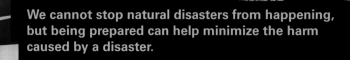

We cannot stop natural disasters from happening, but being prepared can help minimize the harm caused by a disaster.

What Are Natural Disasters?

Natural disasters are nature's most damaging events. They include wildfires, earthquakes, extreme storms, floods, tsunamis (say *soon-ah-meez*), and volcanic eruptions.

Preparing for Natural Disasters

Preparing for natural disasters helps us to reduce their effects in three key ways, by:
- increasing our chances of survival
- making our homes as disaster-proof as possible
- reducing the long-term effects of the disaster.

WILDFIRES

Wildfires are one of the fastest-moving, deadliest natural disasters. They start as small fires but can very quickly grow into large, dangerous wildfires. These fires can move fast, so people who have prepared in advance and know how to react have a far better chance of surviving them than those who have not.

What Are Wildfires?

Wildfires are fires that happen in scrub and forest lands. They can reach temperatures of more than 1,470 °F (800 °C), and may travel faster than people can escape them. Most wildfires occur naturally, but some are deliberately lit by people who want to cause damage.

Preparing for Wildfires

There are three key ways to prepare for a wildfire. You must know:

- the conditions in which wildfires start, and how to act in response
- the safest places to be if a wildfire threatens
- the challenges facing those who survive.

EYEWITNESS WORDS

In June 2010, wildfires in Quebec, Canada, were so intense that Montreal resident Paul Napoli could smell the smoke from more than 200 kilometres away:

"We were sure something was going up in flames …. I'd never smelled anything so intense, even from a fire much closer."

Wildfires and Bushfires

In some countries, such as Australia, wildfires are called bushfires.

In February, 2009, the Black Saturday wildfires raged through Victoria, Australia, claiming the lives of nearly 200 people and injuring more than 400.

WHERE DO WILDFIRES HAPPEN?

*Wildfires are most common in areas of the world called "wildfire zones." These are places where the vegetation and **climate** create the ideal conditions for a wildfire to start and rapidly spread. Increasing numbers of people are choosing to live in wildfire zones because they are often areas of great natural beauty.*

Wildfire Zones

Wildfire zones occur mainly in two bands that stretch around Earth, north and south of the **Tropics**. Here, plants are dried out by warm winters and hot, dry summers. The hot, windy weather in which wildfires happen is common in these areas. However, wildfires can happen outside these areas if the weather and plant life are suited to wildfire conditions.

Matheson Fire
Canada, 1916
273 deaths

Kursha-2 Fire
Russia, 1936
Estimated 1,200 deaths

North America

Europe

Asia

Greater Hinggan Forest Fire
China, 1987
213 deaths

Landes Mountain Fire
France, 1949
230 deaths

Africa

Cloquet Fire
United States, 1918
453 deaths

South America

Key

Fire detections

Sumatra and Kalimantan Fires
Indonesia, 1997
240 deaths

Tropic of Capricorn

Australia

0   2,000 miles
0   2,000 km

Black Saturday
Australia, 2009
173 deaths

Antarctica

N

This map shows the areas of the world where wildfires are most common, and the locations of the seven deadliest fires between 1910 and 2010.

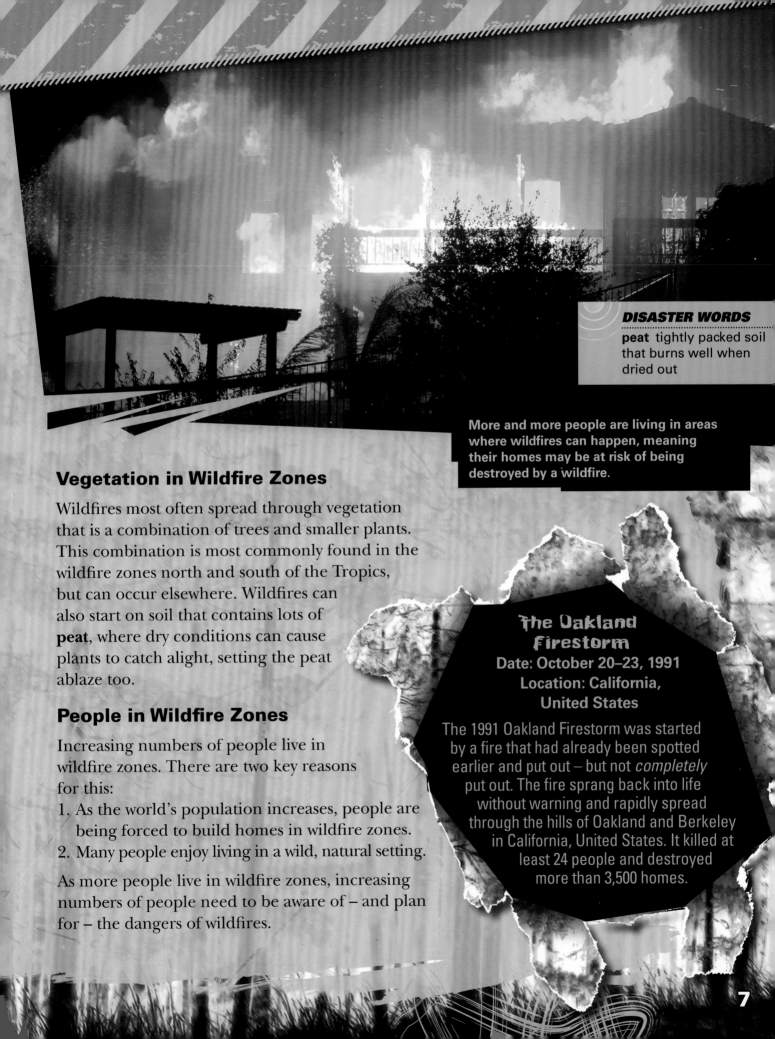

More and more people are living in areas where wildfires can happen, meaning their homes may be at risk of being destroyed by a wildfire.

Vegetation in Wildfire Zones

Wildfires most often spread through vegetation that is a combination of trees and smaller plants. This combination is most commonly found in the wildfire zones north and south of the Tropics, but can occur elsewhere. Wildfires can also start on soil that contains lots of **peat**, where dry conditions can cause plants to catch alight, setting the peat ablaze too.

People in Wildfire Zones

Increasing numbers of people live in wildfire zones. There are two key reasons for this:
1. As the world's population increases, people are being forced to build homes in wildfire zones.
2. Many people enjoy living in a wild, natural setting.

As more people live in wildfire zones, increasing numbers of people need to be aware of – and plan for – the dangers of wildfires.

The Oakland Firestorm
Date: October 20–23, 1991
Location: California, United States

The 1991 Oakland Firestorm was started by a fire that had already been spotted earlier and put out – but not *completely* put out. The fire sprang back into life without warning and rapidly spread through the hills of Oakland and Berkeley in California, United States. It killed at least 24 people and destroyed more than 3,500 homes.

WHAT CAUSES WILDFIRES?

*Wildfires are usually caused by a long period of dry weather, which dries vegetation and provides fires with fuel. For this reason, wildfires often happen in the drier months during summer and fall, or during a **drought.** Increased demands on the world's water resources are making wildfire conditions more common.*

Dry Fuel

Wildfires cannot start without dry fuel. The fuel is made up of plants such as grasses, bushes, and trees that hold little or no moisture. Wildfires are most likely to start and spread on land covered in dry grasses, shrubs, and trees.

This map shows the locations of the wildfires that affected Africa in 2002. They occurred on the fringe between the desert and moist areas, where dried-up plants and trees are common.

Dry, desert areas do not have many plants or trees, so there is no fuel for wildfires.

Green, moist areas have plenty of rain, so plants do not dry out and wildfires cannot start.

Key

◼ Wildfires

Large areas of plants and grasses are drying out due to global warming and the increased demand for water. This provides more fuel for wildfires.

Drought

Water stored in soil and rock is called **groundwater**. It provides plants and trees with moisture during periods of dry weather. However, people are now using this groundwater for household and agricultural purposes. As a result, plants and trees dry out more quickly.

Global Warming

Global warming is the name given to the rise in Earth's average temperature. Most scientists agree wildfires have started affecting areas that were free of wildfires in the past. This will happen as the climate bands in which wildfires often happen shift farther from the **equator**.

DISASTER WORDS

groundwater water stored in soil and rock

equator imaginary line running around the middle of Earth

EYEWITNESS WORDS

David Gillett fought fires in Anakie, Victoria, Australia, in 2009:

"We've had 12 years of drought. The rain that does come produces grasses that are highly flammable. The fuel has been heated over the last month, with record high temperatures. We've had very strong northerly winds and low humidity. It's a recipe for disaster."

HOW DO WILDFIRES START?

Every large, raging wildfire starts as a small fire. These begin in a variety of ways, some caused by nature, others by people. Once a fire has started, warm air, oxygen, and wind will fan the flames, making the fire grow if there is fuel available.

Natural Causes

In nature, fires are usually caused by lightning, volcanic eruptions, or sparks from rock falls. Of these, lightning is the most common cause of fires.

Human Causes

People are responsible for starting many wildfires. The key ways in which this happens are:

- dropping lit cigarettes and starting fires accidentally
- using electrical equipment, motors, or power lines that cause sparks
- leaving campfires without putting them out properly
- starting fires deliberately to clear land of plants and grasses, then not being able to control the fire
- lighting a fire deliberately to cause damage (this is called **arson**).

DISASTER WORDS

arson deliberately starting a fire hoping that it will cause damage

These fires were deliberately lit to clear away undergrowth. They will be safe as long as they are carefully controlled.

10

Even without help from the wind, fires such as this one in Idaho, United States, can travel through trees at more than 6 miles (10 km) per hour and through grasses at more than 12 miles (20 km) per hour.

Small Fires that Grow

Once a fire has sprung up, it is not guaranteed to turn into a wildfire. It requires two further elements for the fire to take hold:

- Warm air must have dried plants and trees until they are **flammable**, otherwise without this fuel the fire will not spread.
- Windy conditions bringing fresh supplies of oxygen to help the fire burn. They also help the fire to spread more rapidly, making it harder for firefighters to control.

The Black Saturday Fires
Date: February 7 to mid-March, 2009
Location: Victoria, Australia

On Saturday February 7, Victoria experienced some of its worst wildfire conditions ever. Temperatures were almost 122 °F (50 °C), and there were winds of more than 60 miles (100 km) per hour. Fires began throughout Victoria, and continued to burn for more than a month. Thousands of homes were destroyed or damaged and 173 people died.

WHAT HAPPENS DURING A WILDFIRE?

Once a wildfire has started, the fire's heat dries out the vegetation in front of it, and draws in oxygen to help it keep burning. At the same time, winds push the flames forward.

The Course of the Wildfire

A wildfire's course is mainly decided by the wind direction. The wind pushes the flames forward and provides the fire with the oxygen that allows it to burn. Wind direction can change very quickly and with little warning. This is one of the things that makes wildfires so dangerous.

The Fire Front

When a wildfire gets large enough, it forms a line of flames called a **fire front**. The heat of the fire front dries out the vegetation in front of it. As the vegetation gets hotter, the trees and plants release flammable gases, which **ignite**. Finally, the trees and other plants become so hot that they burst into flames. Once the fire reaches high enough temperatures, this process happens very quickly, allowing the fire to spread with terrifying speed.

A fire front advances through San Diego, United States.

The heat from a 2009 wildfire in Los Angeles, United States, created a stack effect, carrying huge clouds of smoke high into the air.

The Stack Effect

Large fires create what is called a **stack effect**. As hot air from the fire front rises, colder air from in front of the fire is pulled in, providing the fire with fresh oxygen. As the fire's heat increases, this movement can create a whirl of rising air, spinning around with the force of a tornado.

DISASTER WORDS

stack effect cycle of fast-rising air above a fire front

New Fires

New fires may begin far from the fire front. The wind can carry away burning material that causes spot fires, and super-heated tree trunks can suddenly burst into flames. Sometimes the soil itself may continue to burn below the surface, and the fire can spring back into life hours or days later.

EYEWITNESS WORDS

Frank Bagheri left his Los Angeles home during the 2009 wildfires:

"We finally left because I stopped one of the firefighters running around our street … I wanted to ask him whether the fire would go the other way, or if we'd be OK. He just looked at me and said, 'You don't want to stay here and get trapped.' That phrase – stay here and get trapped – did it. I changed my mind at that point to leave."

WHAT DAMAGE DO WILDFIRES CAUSE?

Wildfires burn at temperatures of more than 1,470 °F (800 °C), and can affect huge areas of land, causing extensive damage to people, animals, and the natural environment.

Human Impact

Wildfires affect people in two key ways: by injuring and killing people, and by damaging property.

Injuring and Killing People

For people, the most serious effect of a wildfire is loss of life. Every year wildfires claim new victims: people who were unprepared, or people who were unlucky enough to be caught by a fire and unable to escape.

Damaging Property

Wildfires cause terrible damage to property. Wildfires can wipe out homes, cars, farms, and even whole towns. This damage can devastate entire communities and their economies. The cost of rebuilding can run into millions of dollars.

 EYEWITNESS WORDS

As Peter Mitchell found out during the Kinglake wildfires in Victoria, Australia, in 2009, even with the best warning systems, fires can arrive unexpectedly:

"I had five seconds' notice and all my fire plans went out of the window. Despite all my preparation, I couldn't save [my home]."

Wildfires raged through California in 2008. In December, some people returned to the area to sift through the debris that was left after the wildfires destroyed their homes.

Environmental Impact

Wildfires affect the natural environment and the animals that depend on it for survival.

Damage to the Environment

Vegetation in wildfire zones is usually well suited to wildfire conditions and can recover quickly. However, if the vegetation is burned away too often, the roots that hold the soil in place may be destroyed. The wind then blows away the soil, leaving the land bare and **barren**. When trees are burned, the carbon in them is released into the atmosphere as carbon dioxide. Once there, it helps trap the sun's heat, adding to **global warming** and making wildfires more likely.

Animals and Wildfires

Many animals live in wildfire zones. When a wildfire occurs, these animals may be caught in the fires and die. Some surviving animals are at risk even after a wildfire, when they can die from burns, dehydration, or lack of food.

DISASTER WORDS

barren unable to support life

global warming an increase in Earth's temperature

Although volunteers are able to help some animals after a wildfire, getting food, water, and medical help to all of them is impossible.

The Kalimantan and Sumatra Fires
Date: July–November 1997
Location: Kalimantan and Sumatra, Indonesia

The Kalimantan and Sumatra fires began as fires to clear land for agriculture. The fires burned out of control and the smoke cloud eventually covered 1,158,300 square miles (3 million sq km).

FORECASTING WILDFIRES

Although no one can forecast a wildfire, the authorities in wildfire zones are aware of the conditions in which one is most likely to start. Based on these conditions, they assess the risk and issue warnings of the danger level.

Assessing Wildfire Risk

Authorities monitor risk factors to help them forecast the likelihood of a wildfire. This likelihood depends on two key elements: local environmental and weather conditions, and the time of day.

Local Conditions

Wildfires are most likely to start in dry vegetation during hot, windy weather. The more extreme each of these three conditions is, the more likely it becomes that a wildfire will start.

Time of Day

Fires are most likely to start and spread rapidly when temperatures are high. This means they are least likely to start at night, when temperatures are lowest. Fires are most likely to start in the late afternoon, after the sun has been warming the air all day.

Wildfire authorities can help people to stay alert for potential wildfires by observing the local conditions.

The Peloponnese Fires
Date: August 23–mid September, 2007
Location: Peloponnese Peninsula, Greece

The Peloponnese fires were the worst of a series of forest fires that hit Greece during the unusually dry summer and fall of 2007. Almost 100 people died, several of them firefighters. More than 104,250 square miles (270,000 sq km) of land was destroyed.

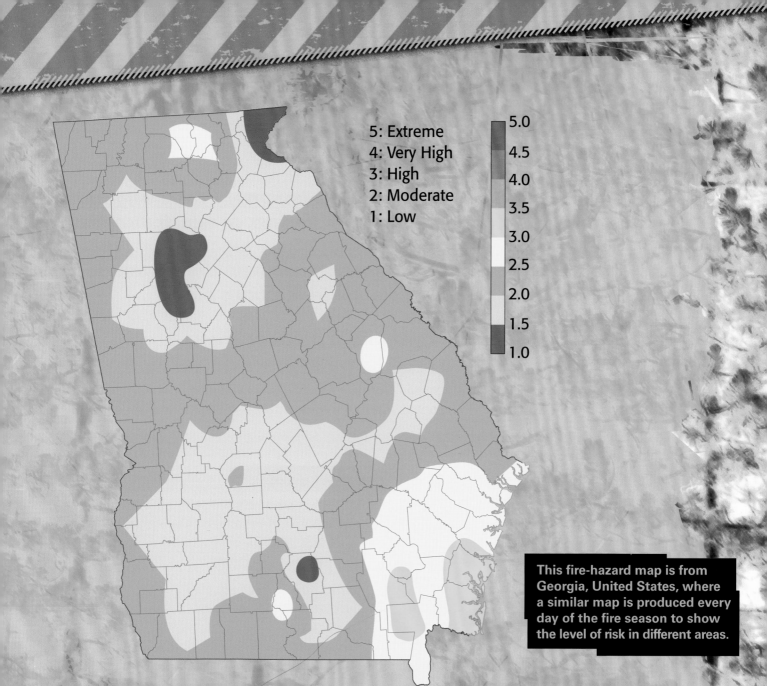

5: Extreme
4: Very High
3: High
2: Moderate
1: Low

5.0
4.5
4.0
3.5
3.0
2.5
2.0
1.5
1.0

This fire-hazard map is from Georgia, United States, where a similar map is produced every day of the fire season to show the level of risk in different areas.

Computer Modeling

Firefighting services use computer modeling to help work out how fires might spread. They can use this information to decide where to concentrate their fire-prevention work. Computers are also used to produce fire-hazard maps, which show the areas in most danger from wildfires.

Warnings

In areas where wildfires are likely to occur, the authorities monitor the level of danger and post regular warnings. The warnings are often presented as a scale showing people how **vigilant** they need to be. The warnings may also restrict specific types of fires, such as barbecues or campfires.

DISASTER WORDS
vigilant watchful and alert

MONITORING WILDFIRES

Once a wildfire has started, it is important for firefighters and others to know how it will behave. In which direction is the fire spreading? How quickly? How high and fast-moving are the flames? This information will help firefighters to fight the fire and warn people in the fire's path.

Monitoring Wildfire Direction

Wildfires are blown forward by the wind, and this affects their direction and speed. Weather forecasters monitor how wind direction and speed are changing, but predicting how wind will influence a fire's direction is never 100 percent accurate.

EYEWITNESS WORDS

Guy Lamothe's property in Oakridge, Victoria, Australia, was saved from a 2009 bushfire when the wind suddenly changed direction:

'The cool change saved us …. The fire was one kilometre (half a mile) away, but then the wind direction shifted [from the north] to the south.'

wind direction

fire front

The spread of a wildfire from its starting place is determined by wind speed and direction.

Wildfires change their size and speed as they cross hilly country.

Monitoring Wildfire Behavior

As the fire services monitor a fire's progress, they look ahead at the **topography** of the ground it is heading for. Topography influences a fire's speed and the height of its flames.

Speed

Fires tend to move quickest when they are going uphill. The super-hot air in front of the fire rises up the slope, rapidly heating the vegetation. For the same reason, fires usually move more slowly when going downhill.

Flame Height

When a fire heading downhill hits flat land, the flames can suddenly become up to four times as high. When they hit an uphill section, they become four times as high again. This means that even a relatively small 18-inch (0.5-m) downhill fire can become a 26-foot (8-m) wall of flame within minutes, as it shifts from traveling downhill to across flat land and then to traveling uphill.

DISASTER WORDS
topography arrangement of hills and valleys on the land

The Peshtigo Fire
Date: October 8, 1871
Location:
Wisconsin/Michigan,
United States

The Peshtigo fire was the worst wildfire ever to hit North America. Strong winds fanned small fires, which grew rapidly until 1,873 square miles (3,000 sq km) of land had been burned. The fire caught many people by surprise and up to 2,500 people died.

WHEN A WILDFIRE STRIKES

Almost every wildfire that starts is safely brought under control before it causes terrible damage. When a wildfire does threaten an area, it is important that firefighters detect and tackle the fire as quickly as possible.

DISASTER WORDS

infrared cameras
cameras that photograph heat rays

EYEWITNESS WORDS

Katerina Papatryfon Drakopoulis witnessed the 2009 wildfires that threatened Athens, Greece:

"The fires are crazy. Just when you think they have been put out, the flames rise again and keep going."

Detecting the Fire

There are various ways of detecting a wildfire. The simplest is for firefighters to climb a tower and look for smoke. They can either rush to put out the fire or call for help. Today, wealthy countries also use faster, more technologically advanced fire-alert systems:

- **Infrared cameras** detect hot spots, which show that a fire has started.
- Satellite images reveal unusual amounts of smoke in unpopulated areas.
- Computer systems immediately send out warnings to the emergency services if hot spots or smoke are discovered.

Satellite photos of wildfires, such as this one in Southern California in 2007, provide early warning that a fire has begun and help to indicate the direction in which it is spreading. Firefighters then know where to concentrate their efforts.

Special planes can be used to drop chemicals onto wildfires, which helps to stop them from spreading.

Fire-Prevention Techniques

Fire-prevention techniques aim to deprive fires of fuel, so there is less chance that fires will start, or spread. They include:

- clearing undergrowth
- carefully burning vegetation in areas where fires are likely to start
- cutting down trees and other vegetation to create a gap called a **firebreak**, which a fire will be unable to cross.

Firefighting Techniques

Once a fire has taken hold, the firefighting services have a range of techniques. They may:

- use water or **fire-retardant chemicals** to **douse** the flames
- use water to wet down fuel that lies in the fire's path
- burn or clear a firebreak in the fire's path.

The Ash Wednesday Fires
Date: February 16, 1983
Location: South Australia/ Victoria, Australia

The Ash Wednesday fires in Australia occurred when more than 180 fires blazed into life on the same day. The number and size of the fires overwhelmed the emergency services. Seventy-five people died, many when strong winds suddenly pushed the fires in a completely new direction.

ARE YOU AT RISK?

Are you and your family at risk from wildfires? Your local library and council offices, and the Internet, are good places to start to investigate the area where you are living or staying.

Key Questions

Measure the risk from wildfires by asking key questions about an area's wildfire history, and whether there are preparations in place in case a wildfire breaks out. Ask the following questions about where you live, or where you are holidaying.

Are You in a Wildfire Zone?

Your local council will know about wildfire zones. They will have a map showing the different levels of overall risk in the local area. If you live in a wildfire zone, there may also be daily or weekly fire-hazard maps that show how high the risks are.

The Miramichi Fire
Date: October, 1825
Location: New Brunswick, Canada and Maine, United States

The Miramichi fire occurred in an era before fire warnings. It killed at least 160 people, and burned out 4,633 square miles (12,000 sq km). One of the worst events was at the town of Newcastle in New Brunswick, Canada: in three hours, 248 of the town's 260 buildings burned down.

SMOKEY

FIRE DANGER

HIGH

TODAY!

Look out for warning signs saying you are in a wildfire zone.

PREVENT WILDFIRES

The owners of this house survived because they had done everything they could to make the house fire-safe.

Has Your Area Ever Been Affected by Wildfires Before?

If wildfires have happened before, there is a high risk of them happening again. Even if they have not happened before, wildfires could still occur. Changes to vegetation or climate may mean wildfires could now happen.

Has There Been a Heatwave or a Drought?

Heatwaves and droughts increase the risk of wildfires, as vegetation dries out and is more likely to catch fire. Key signs that vegetation is drying out include trees dropping their leaves out of season, and wells and rivers drying up.

Have You Reduced the Risk of Wildfire Damage Around Your Home?

If a wildfire does come your way, any preparations you have made beforehand will lower the risk of the fire affecting your home. However, some fires happen so quickly and are so powerful that the best thing to do is to **evacuate**.

DISASTER WORDS

evacuate leave a dangerous area

EYEWITNESS WORDS

US firefighter Tom Watson knows how unpredictable wildfires can be:

"I'd rather fight 100 [house] fires than a [wild]fire. With a structure fire you know where your flames are, but in the woods it can move anywhere; it can come right up behind you."

TOP TIPS FOR REDUCING RISK

If you live in a wildfire zone, the risk of a wildfire can never be completely removed. However, the risks can be reduced if you prepare properly for when a wildfire threatens.

Reducing Risk Around the Home

When preparing your home for the wildfire season, follow the guidelines on page 25 to reduce the threat from the fire and **embers**. Make your house "fire ready" even if you are planning to **evacuate**, in case you are unable to evacuate.

Preparing an Emergency Plan

Your wildfire plan outlines what each person in your family will do if a wildfire threatens your community. You need to know:

- where everyone will meet up if a fire threatens
- who to contact (and how) if the family gets separated
- the location of your family's wildfire emergency kit
- what job everyone will do if a wildfire draws near your home and you cannot evacuate.

Wildfire Emergency Kit

Keep a wildfire emergency kit somewhere easily accessible. It should contain the things you will need if a wildfire strikes, including:
- wind-up radio and wind-up torch
- freshwater and canned food to last several days
- cutlery, plates, and can-opener
- protective clothing
- essential documents and valuables
- first-aid kit.

Wildfire Myths

Believing some of these myths about wildfires could cost you your life.

1 *The most dangerous part of a wildfire is the flames.*

False! The most dangerous part of a wildfire is actually the heat that travels in front of the fire. If you are unprotected, it can kill you instantly.

2 *If you are in a car, you can outrun a wildfire.*

False! Wildfires move incredibly quickly. Getting away in a car can be difficult because fallen trees can block roads and smoke can make it difficult to see.

3 *Only people who live in forests are at risk during wildfires.*

False! People who live in towns, on the coast, close to grass, or farmland, and on the outskirts of cities can also be affected by wildfires. Everyone needs to be aware of fire danger and have a fire action plan.

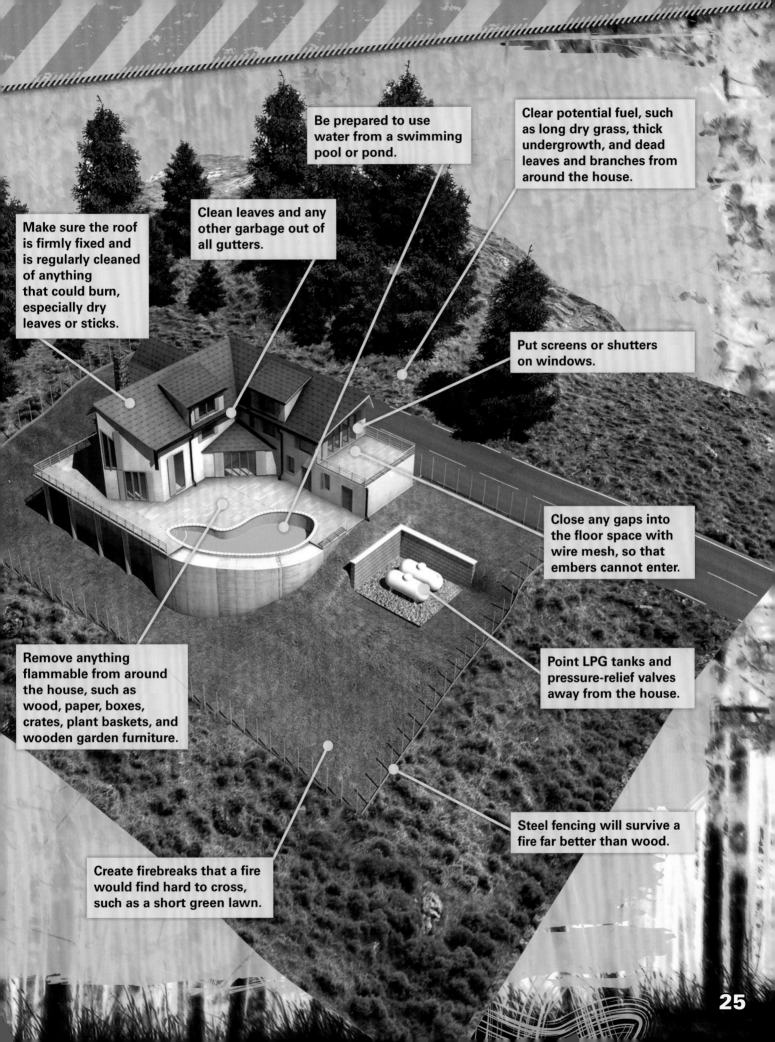

Be prepared to use water from a swimming pool or pond.

Clear potential fuel, such as long dry grass, thick undergrowth, and dead leaves and branches from around the house.

Clean leaves and any other garbage out of all gutters.

Make sure the roof is firmly fixed and is regularly cleaned of anything that could burn, especially dry leaves or sticks.

Put screens or shutters on windows.

Close any gaps into the floor space with wire mesh, so that embers cannot enter.

Remove anything flammable from around the house, such as wood, paper, boxes, crates, plant baskets, and wooden garden furniture.

Point LPG tanks and pressure-relief valves away from the house.

Steel fencing will survive a fire far better than wood.

Create firebreaks that a fire would find hard to cross, such as a short green lawn.

WHAT YOU CAN DO IF A WILDFIRE HAPPENS

*When a wildfire starts in your area, the first decision to make is whether or not to **evacuate**. If your family decides (or is forced) to stay, there are plenty of things you can do together to fight the fire and defend your home.*

Evacuation

Sometimes, the authorities advise people to evacuate to a safer place. People may also make their own decision to leave, without being told. It is important to:

- Make the decision early. Many people who die in wildfires are caught during last-minute evacuations.
- Remember that official advice is based on expert opinions of how the fire will behave.
- Try always to use evacuation routes that you have been told will be safe.
- Listen to updates before and during evacuation.

These cars are evacuating from a wildfire area. With the fire so close and smoke all around, it would have been safer to evacuate sooner.

Being caught in a car during a wildfire is very dangerous. If you are at home and a wildfire is near, it is better to stay and defend your property than to try and escape in a car.

Defending Your Home

If your family needs to defend your home against a wildfire, use the time before it arrives to prepare. This gives you the maximum chance of survival once the fire arrives.

As the Fire Draws Near

Keep track of the fire's progress by listening to the radio. You should also:

- dress in protective clothing and drink water frequently
- wet down the roof, garden, and house walls, especially on the side nearest the fire. Block **downpipes**, and use a hose to fill the gutters with water
- if possible, turn on garden sprinklers
- fill baths, sinks, and buckets with water, for drinking and putting out small fires.

When the Fire Is Close by

When the fire draws near, go inside. Close windows and doors, and use wet towels and blankets to block any gaps under doors and windows. Close heavy curtains and shutters: this will stop smoke getting in.

AFTER A WILDFIRE

The danger from a wildfire has not passed when the **fire front** moves on. It is still possible for the fire to spring back into life hours or even days later. Communities need to work together to make the area safe and make sure everyone has food, water, and shelter.

Help after the Disaster

DISASTER WORDS

fire front the leading edge of a moving fire

After a wildfire, it is important for local communities to work together, sharing crucial supplies and recovering from the fire's effects.

Food, Water, and Shelter

Some people may have lost their homes or all their possessions. They will need food, water, shelter, and clothing.

EYEWITNESS WORDS

Thomas Legrary gave shelter to neighbors whose houses had burned down in the 2009 Kinglake wildfire, Victoria, Australia:

"I've got four families with me at the moment in my house ... I know probably 20 people who have lost their houses, and I haven't ventured out from my place very far at all."

Make the Area Safe

People will also need to work together to make the area safe or to indicate hazards. For example, poisonous chemicals may have been released, electrical lines may be damaged and dangerous, and buildings may be unstable.

The terrible wildfires that hit Victoria, Australia in February 2009, destroyed many people's homes, so they had to live in emergency shelters around the state.

Spot fires can burn long after the danger from the main fire has passed. Firefighters need to patrol the wildfire area to make sure all spot fires are put out.

Remain Vigilant

Its important to remain **vigilant** for at least 24 hours after a wildfire has passed, in case the fire starts up again. Your family and friends should:

- patrol the home and garden, looking for spot fires started by **embers** that have landed on unburned vegetation
- make frequent checks for embers that might have got into roof spaces or other hidden areas
- wet down roofs and any other flammable materials near houses, to stop fire catching there
- wet down ash and debris with a fine spray to help clear the air
- wear protective clothing, if possible. Wear a dust mask, too, as the air is likely to be full of ash containing harmful chemicals.

The Kursha-2 Fires

Date: August, 1936
Location: Ryazan Oblast, Russia

Kursha-2 was a logging settlement in Russia until it was hit in August, 1936 by one of the world's deadliest known wildfire. Warned that the fire was coming, women and children tried to escape by train, but a railway bridge caught fire. An estimated 1,200 people died. There were only 20 survivors, who had sheltered in wells, a pond, and on an open hillside.

QUIZ: DO YOU KNOW WHAT TO DO?

Now that you have read about wildfires, do you feel you would have a better chance of survival? Test yourself using this quiz.

1 When is a wildfire most likely to happen?

a During a long spell of extremely hot weather
b During the daytime
c Both of the above.

2 How should you prepare your garden if you live in a wildfire area?

a Get lots of plants that can regenerate after a fire
b Keep the grass nice and green
c Clear away dead bushes and make sure the distance between the house and anything that could burn is as wide as possible.

3 In a wildfire, who is in the most danger?

a The elderly and the very young
b People trapped in burning houses
c Those who **evacuate** at the last minute and get caught by the flames.

4 What should you do to the gutters of your house as a wildfire approaches?

a Pull them off, in case they catch fire
b Paint them white to reflect the heat
c Block up the **downpipes**, so that the gutters fill with water as you wet down the roof.

5 What is the biggest danger once the fire front has passed?

a Tree trunks that explode because they got too hot in the flames
b Burning your feet on the hot ground
c Spot fires and **embers** that will cause the fire to spring back to life.

How did you do?

Mostly a or b answers: If you are planning on spending time in a wildfire zone, you had better read this book again. At the moment, you would be in great danger!

Mostly or all c answers: Not only would you have the best possible chance of surviving, you might also be able to help other people stay safer during a wildfire.

DISASTER WORDS

evacuate leave a dangerous area

downpipes drainpipes leading from the roof to ground level

fire front the leading edge of a moving fire

embers glowing particles that "shower" down from a fire

DISASTER WATCHING ON THE WEB

Being on disaster watch means being prepared. It also means knowing where to get information ahead of a disaster, knowing how disasters happen, receiving disaster warnings, and getting updates on what is happening after a disaster has struck.

Find out More about Wildfires

Check out these web sites to find out more about wildfires.

- **www.howstuffworks.com**
  Searching this site using the term "wildfire" will lead to all kinds of information on how fires start, protecting your home, what to do if a fire traps you, and how investigators work out whether a fire was deliberately started.
- **www.weatherwizkids.com**
  This site has good basic information on how fires start, where they happen, and "fire tornadoes," as well as fighting fires.
- **www.clearlyexplained.com**
  This site has basic information about bushfires (another term for wildfires), and is particularly good on how wildfires affect the environment.

Wildfires near you

How would a wildfire affect your local area, and what warning might you get? To find out, contact your local government and see whether:

- they have a wildfire emergency plan and maps of wildfire zones
- they know of a web site you can look at for wildfire warnings.

Your local library might also be able to help you find this information. Alternatively, this web site might be able to provide you with local information:

- **www.weather.gov** The US National Weather Service carries a live map showing all kinds of weather-related hazards (including flooding) in the United States.

INDEX